FUN FACTS ABOUT
SNAKES!

Carmen Bredeson

Enslow Elementary

an imprint of

Enslow Publishers, Inc.

40 Industrial Road
Box 398
Berkeley Heights, NJ 07922
USA

http://www.enslow.com

CONTENTS

WORDS TO KNOW

prey (PRAY)—An animal that is food for another animal.

python (PYE thahn)—A very big snake that squeezes its prey.

scales (SKAILZ)—Hard pieces on the skin of many fish and reptiles.

venom (VEH nuhm)—A liquid from an animal that causes sickness or death.

PARTS OF A SNAKE

Western Diamondback Rattlesnake

head
eye
tongue
scale
tail
body

WHERE DO SNAKES LIVE?

Sonoran Mountain
Kingsnake

Snakes like to hide.
Some crawl into
deep holes or
climb trees.
Others live in
oceans or lakes.
All snakes like
warm places best.
If a snake gets
too cold, it
cannot move.

5

DO SNAKES MAKE SOUNDS?

Most snakes are very, very quiet.
Some hiss to let us know they are close.
A rattlesnake shakes its tail to tell us to
stay away. *Rattle*. *Rattle*. When you hear
that sound, it is time to leave.

Western Diamondback Rattlesnake

A Two-striped Forest Pit Viper shows her sharp teeth to guard her baby.

HOW DO SNAKES
KILL THEIR PREY?

Snakes have very sharp teeth. The teeth point back so the snake can hold its **prey**. Some snakes have teeth that can shoot **venom** into the prey. Other snakes squeeze their prey to kill it.

A Rock Python chokes its prey.

WHAT DO SNAKES EAT?

Snakes eat animals such as mice, birds, frogs, and worms. Big snakes even eat goats and small deer. Snakes do not chew their food.

Common Egg-eater

They swallow it whole. Strong muscles slowly push the food down into the snake's stomach.

Broad-banded Copperhead

Checkered Garter Snake

HOW DO SNAKES SMELL AND TASTE?

A snake flicks its tongue in and out, in and out. The tongue brings air into the mouth. Places in the snake's mouth test the air. The snake's brain can tell what is in the air.

HOW DO SNAKES SHED THEIR SKIN?

Egyptian Banded Cobra with shed skin

Snakes grow new skin when their old skin gets too small. The snake rubs on a rock to make a tiny crack in its skin. The crack gets bigger and bigger. As the snake crawls, the old skin comes off in one piece.

14

15

King Snake

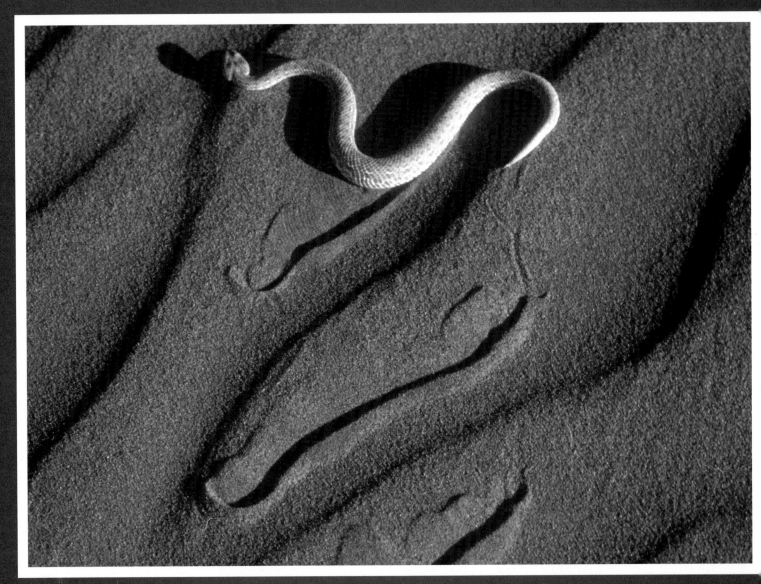

This sidewinding Peringuey's Adder leaves tracks in the sand.

HOW DO **SNAKES** MOVE?

Snakes have tough pieces on their skin called **scales**. The scales hold onto the ground. Muscles push the snake's body along. A sidewinder snake moves by throwing its body sideways. Almost all snakes can swim, too.

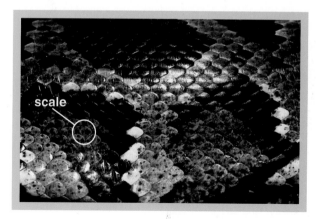

scale

Scales on a Burmese Python

WHICH IS THE BIGGEST SNAKE?
WHICH IS THE SMALLEST?

Brahminy Blind Snakes can fit in your hand. The lighter one will soon shed its skin.

One kind of **python** can grow to be more than 30 feet long. It would take about eight of you to be that tall. Blind snakes are the smallest snakes. They can be as short and thin as a toothpick.

The Reticulated Python is the longest snake in the world.

WHAT IS THE LIFE CYCLE OF A SNAKE?

1. Most snakes hatch from eggs.

2. Each little snake has an egg tooth. The sharp tooth helps break the egg from the inside.

3. This Indian Rock Python is all grown up.

LEARN MORE

BOOKS

Gunzi, Christiane. *The Best Book of Snakes*. Boston: Houghton Mifflin, 2006.

Holub, Joan. *Why Do Snakes Hiss?* New York: Penguin Young Readers Group, Puffin Books, 2004.

Parker, Steve. *See-through Reptiles*. Philadelphia: Running Press Kids, 2004.

Chihuahuan Mountain Kingsnake

WEB SITES

Enchanted Learning

<http://www.enchantedlearning.com/subjects/reptiles/snakes/printouts.shtml>

San Diego Zoo

<http://www.sandiegozoo.org/animalbytes/t-rattlesnake.html>

East African Bush Snake

INDEX

Green Bush Viper

A Note About Reptiles and Amphibians:
Amphibians **can live on land or in water. Frogs, toads, and salamanders are amphibians.**
Reptiles **have skin covered with scales. Snakes, alligators, turtles, and lizards are reptiles.**

Enslow Elementary, an imprint of Enslow Publishers, Inc.
Enslow Elementary® is a registered trademark of Enslow Publishers, Inc.

Copyright © 2008 by Carmen Bredeson

Library of Congress Cataloging-in-Publication Data

Bredeson, Carmen.
    Fun facts about snakes! / Carmen Bredeson.
        p. cm. — (I like reptiles and amphibians!)
    Includes bibliographical references and index.
    ISBN-13: 978-0-7660-2787-9
    ISBN-10: 0-7660-2787-2
    1. Snakes—Juvenile literature. I. Title. II. Series.
QL666.O6B74 2007
597.96—dc22   2006015918

Printed in the United States of America

10 9 8 7 6 5 4 3 2 1

Every effort has been made to locate all copyright holders of material used in this
book. If any errors or omissions have occurred, corrections will be made in future
editions of this book.

To Our Readers: We have done our best to make sure all Internet Addresses in this
book were active and appropriate when we went to press. However, the author and the
publisher have no control over and assume no liability for the material available on
those Internet sites or on other Web sites they may link to. Any comments or
suggestions can be sent by e-mail to comments@enslow.com or to the address on the
back cover.

Photo Credits: Craig K. Lorenz / Photo Researchers, Inc., p. 7; Fletcher & Baylis /
Photo Researchers, Inc., p. 19; © G. & C. Merker / Visuals Unlimited, p. 22; © Jim
Merli / Visuals Unlimited, p. 15; © Joe & Mary Ann McDonald / Visuals Unlimited,
p. 20; © Joe McDonald / Visuals Unlimited, pp. 14, 21 (top); Joe Tomoleoni, p. 18;
© John Cancalosi / Naturepl.com, pp. 4–5; © 2006 Jupiterimages Corporation, pp.
1, 11, 17, 23; © Michael Fogden / Animals Animals, p. 16; © Mira / Alamy, p. 21
(bottom); © Nick Greaves / Alamy, p. 10; © Pete Oxford / Naturepl.com, pp. 2, 8; ©
Peter Blackwell / Naturepl.com, p. 9; © Shutterstock, p. 3; © Zigmund Leszczynski /
Animals Animals, p. 12.

Cover Photograph: © Joe McDonald / Tom Stack & Associates

Series Science Consultant:
Raoul Bain
Herpetology Biodiversity Specialist
Center for Biodiversity and
    Conservation
American Museum of Natural History
New York, NY

Series Literacy Consultant:
Allan A. De Fina, Ph.D.
Past President of the New Jersey
    Reading Association
Professor, Department of Literacy Education
New Jersey City University
Jersey City, NJ